To All Children

**Illustrations and Artwork by
Zeinab Shalaby, Hossam El Mouelhi, and Donia Farouk**

Edited by Wafaa Shalaby and Noha Elmouelhi

First edition 2024
ISBN 978-1-959536-08-6

Published by Honey Elm Books LLC
www.HoneyElmBooks.com

IN SHAA ALLAH
إن شاء الله

By: Zeinab Shalaby

Noura is a beautiful girl.

She loves playing with her friends on the playground.

One day after school, she told her friends,

"Tomorrow, we will go to the playground

and have fun together."

Everyone was so happy and looking forward to playing together the next day.

The next day,
it was raining all day long.
Noura could not go to the playground
to meet her friends and play together.

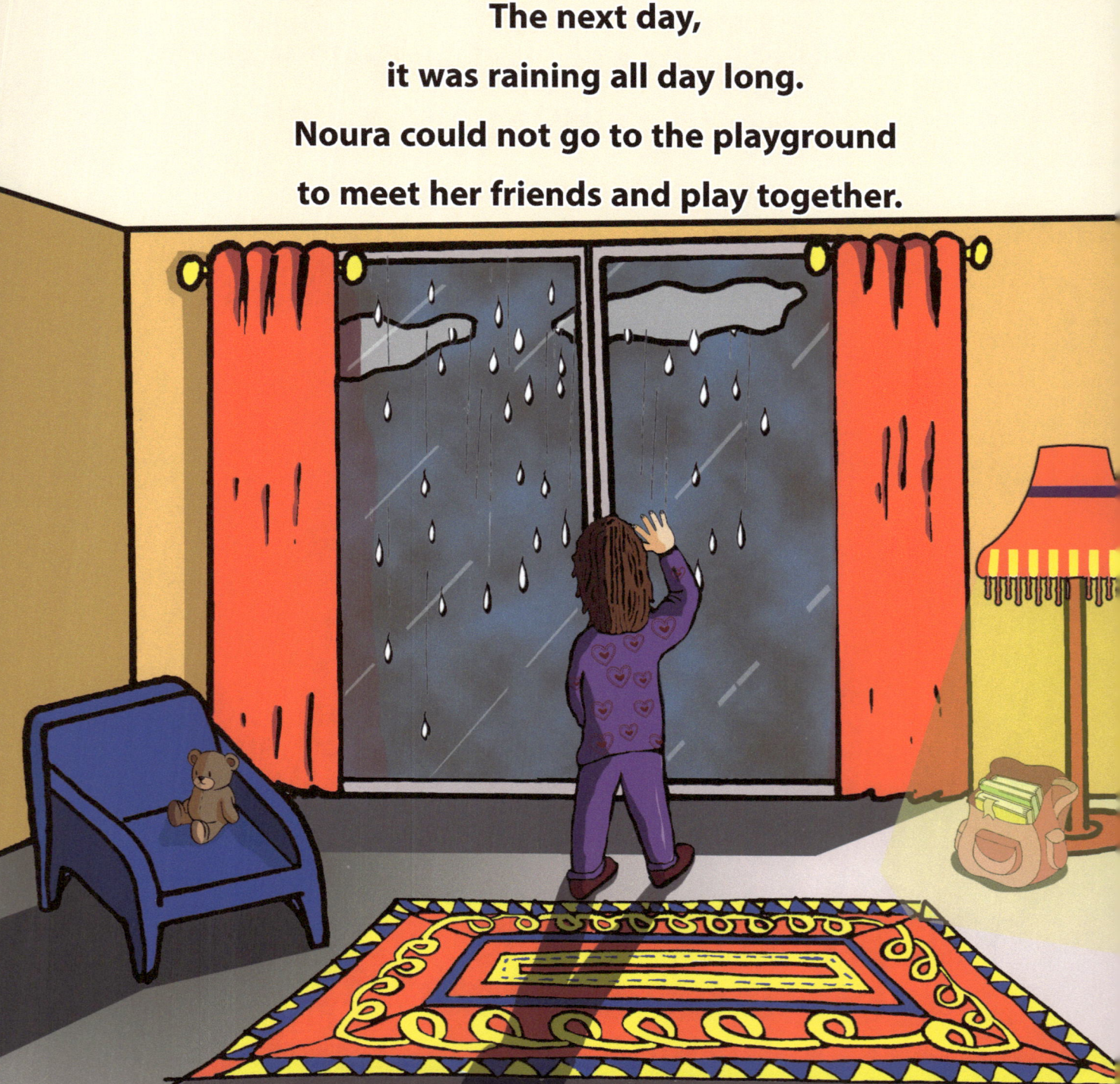

Noura was very sad.

Noura's dad asked her,
"Why are you so sad?"
Noura told her dad that she had promised her friends
to meet at the playground to play together. But it had
been raining all day and now this was not going to happen!

Dad asked Noura,
"Did you say 'In shaa Allah'?"
Noura said,
"No, I did not. I forgot!"

Dad said, "My dear girl,
you know everything happens according to Allah's Will.
Allah Has the best plans for us.

IN SHAA ALLAH

When you say 'In shaa Allah'
when planning anything,
you will always be happy
with whatever might happen.
So, remember 'In shaa Allah.'"

One Friday, Haady told his friends after school,

"Let's meet tomorrow at the park to play soccer."

They were all excited and looking forward
to playing soccer on Saturday.

When Saturday morning came,

Haady woke up with a fever.

He was very sick. Haady could not get out of bed.

Haady was very sad.

He would not be able to go to the park,

nor meet his friends to play soccer.

Haady's mom asked him, "Why are you so sad?"
Haady told his mom about what he had been planning
to do with his friends.
He was sad because he was sick and he would not be able
to have fun with his friends.

Haady's mom asked him,
"Did you say 'In shaa Allah'?"
Haady said,
"No, I did not. I forgot!"

Haady's mom comforted him and told him,

"Dear Haady, you should always say 'In shaa Allah'

whenever you want to do anything.

Allah Has the best plans for us.

IN SHAA ALLAH

When you say 'In shaa Allah'

you will not be sad

if your plan does not work because

you trust that Allah has a better plan."

Remember that everything happens according to Allah's Will.
So, always say "In shaa Allah (God Willing)" when planning anything.
" *IN SHAA ALLAH* "
"إن شاء الله"

www.ingramcontent.com/pod-product-compliance
Lightning Source LLC
Chambersburg PA
CBHW041614120626
46551CB00002B/437